CONFRONTING
Anti-Semitism

KOFI A. ANNAN
ELIE WIESEL

RUDER FINN PRESS

Editorial Director: Susan Slack

Creative Director: Lisa Gabbay

Senior Art Director: Sal Catania

Art Director: Diana Yeo

Production Director: Valerie Thompson

Design: Ruder Finn Design, New York

First published in the United States in 2006 by
Ruder Finn Press, Inc.
301 East 57th Street
New York, NY 10022

1-932646-16-7

Printed in the United States of America by Ruder Finn Printing Services, New York,
Bryan D'Orazio, Senior Vice President

With special thanks to the staff of Ruder Finn Israel and especially to Rashi Elmaliah for her tireless dedication in researching and compiling the images included in this publication.

Cover
Desecrated graves in a Jewish cemetery,
St. Petersburg, Russia,
February 2004

Table of contents

Introduction
Shashi Tharoor, United Nations Under-Secretary-General
for Communications and Public Information   6

Practice Tolerance
Kofi Annan, United Nations Secretary-General   12

We Plead on Behalf of an Ancient People
Elie Wiesel   48

Norway
March 2004

Introduction

SHASHI THAROOR

UNITED NATIONS UNDER-SECRETARY-GENERAL
FOR COMMUNICATIONS AND PUBLIC INFORMATION

Anti-Semitism is a blot on the record of
humanity. As the longest surviving form of
bigotry, it has a long and ugly history. It has
wrought unfathomable havoc and destruction
on millions of ordinary people, not only in the
twentieth century.

Anti-Semitism is not only a problem for
Jews. It is a symptom of a disease that, if not
addressed, will weaken us all; the disease of
intolerance. Intolerance led to global war
twice last century. As George Santayana so
eloquently wrote, "Those who cannot
remember the past are condemned to repeat it."

Many people thought that anti-Semitism had been dealt a death blow with the Allied victory that ended World War II, but it has not gone away. Once again, symbols of hate are being painted on Jewish homes and some people have been obliged to celebrate Hannukah — a festival of lights — behind darkened windows. This is not just wrong, it is unacceptable. And we all have both a responsibility and an interest in stopping it.

In this book, two Nobel Peace Prize Laureates, Mr. Elie Wiesel and United Nations Secretary-General Kofi Annan, issue a clarion call to the United Nations and the peoples of the world to confront this evil.

One great thing about the United Nations is its universal membership. It derives its very legitimacy from the fact that every country in the world is a member, and every newly-independent state seeks entry almost as its first order of governmental business.

Because of this universality, no-one should feel foreign to the United Nations — it belongs to us all — and the United Nations should not feel foreign to anyone.

The diplomats who represent their countries at the United Nations have a responsibility to promote their countries' national interests, but the duty of the Secretariat of the United Nations, led by Secretary-General Annan, is to serve all the peoples of the world. When any people believe that the United Nations does not address their legitimate concerns, we, in the United Nations Secretariat, must raise those concerns, because when people are being attacked on the basis of their culture, their ethnicity or their religion, this is our problem.

On 21 June 2004, the United Nations Secretariat organized the first-ever United Nations seminar on anti-Semitism at United Nations Headquarters. Elie Wiesel once observed that the opposite of hate was not love, but indifference. This event marked, at the very least, the end of indifference at the United Nations.

What will the next step be? Another lesson of the twentieth century is that we should never underestimate the power of constructive, caring, committed people. Ordinary people brought down the Iron Curtain. They drove out dictators, and entrenched the concepts of democracy and human rights in the lexicon of international diplomacy. They are a force to be reckoned with.

With sufficient pressure, encouragement and support from ordinary people, the task of uniting the world's governments to combat anti-Semitism and intolerance should not be beyond diplomats and negotiators.

This small volume reproduces the speeches made by the Secretary-General and Elie Wiesel at the United Nations seminar. They have called on the world's people to do their utmost in the struggle against anti-Semitism and intolerance. I hope readers will be inspired to take up this challenge.

WE KNOW YOU
SHARE OUR
OUTRAGE AT
THIS HATEFUL
ACT. PLEASE
JOIN US AT NOON
MONDAY TO
REPAIR THE
SUKKAH.
(Pizza in the Hut is still on)
WISHING EVERYONE
SHALOM, PEACE...

Sukkah defaced with swastikas,
University of Colorado at Boulder
January 2000

Practice Tolerance

KOFI A. ANNAN

SIXTY YEARS AGO, in adopting the Charter of the United Nations, the world's peoples asserted their determination "to practice tolerance and live together in peace with one another as good neighbors."

No Muslim, no Jew, no Christian, no Hindu, no Buddhist — no one who is true to the principles of any of the world's faiths, no one who claims a cultural, national or religious identity based on values such as truth, decency and justice — can be neutral in the fight against intolerance.

Clearly, our success in this struggle depends on the effort we make to educate ourselves and our children. Intolerance can be unlearnt. Tolerance and mutual respect have to be learnt.

Intolerance is directed at many groups in many parts of the world, notably Muslims and migrants — groups that overlap, but each of which, sadly, encounters prejudice in its own right.

Yet throughout history, anti-Semitism has been a unique manifestation of hatred, intolerance and persecution. Anti-Semitism has flourished even in communities where Jews have never lived, and it has been a harbinger of discrimination against others.

The rise of anti-Semitism anywhere is a threat to people everywhere. Thus, in fighting anti-Semitism we fight for the future of all humanity.

The Shoah, or Holocaust was the epitome of this evil. Germany in the 1930s was a modern society, at the cutting edge of human technical advance and cultural achievement. Yet the Nazi regime that took power set out to exterminate Jews from the face of the earth.

We know — and yet we still cannot really comprehend — that six million innocent Jewish men, women and children were murdered, just because they were Jews. That is a crime against humanity that defies imagination.

The name "United Nations" was coined to describe the alliance fighting to end that barbarous regime, and our Organization came into being when the world had just learnt the full horror of the concentration and extermination camps. It is therefore rightly said that the United Nations emerged from the ashes of the Holocaust. And a human rights agenda that fails to address anti-Semitism denies its own history.

Worldwide revulsion at this terrible genocide was the driving force behind the Universal Declaration of Human Rights. As the Preamble to the Declaration says, "disregard and contempt for human rights have resulted in barbarous acts which have outraged the conscience of mankind." And it was no coincidence that, on the day before it adopted the Declaration in 1948, the General Assembly had adopted the

Convention on the Prevention and
Punishment of the Crime of Genocide.

It is hard to believe that, 60 years after
the tragedy of the Holocaust, anti-Semitism
is once again rearing its head. But it is clear
that we are witnessing an alarming resurgence
of this phenomenon in new forms and
manifestations. This time, the world must
not, cannot, be silent.

We owe it to ourselves, as well as to our
Jewish brothers and sisters, to stand firmly
against the particular tide of hatred that anti-
Semitism represents. And that means we must
be prepared to examine the nature of today's
manifestations of anti-Semitism more closely.

Let us acknowledge that the United
Nations' record on anti-Semitism has at
times fallen short of our ideals. The General

Assembly resolution of 1975, equating Zionism with racism, was an especially unfortunate decision. I am glad that it has since been rescinded.

But there remains a need for constant vigilance. So let us actively and uncompromisingly refute those who seek to deny the fact of the Holocaust or its uniqueness, or who continue to spread lies and vile stereotypes about Jews and Judaism.

When we seek justice for the Palestinians — as we must — let us firmly disavow anyone who tries to use that cause to incite hatred against Jews, in Israel or elsewhere.

The human rights machinery of the United Nations has been mobilized in the battle against anti-Semitism, and this must continue. I urge the special rapporteurs on religious freedom and on contemporary racism, working with the Office of the High Commissioner for Human Rights (which has recently strengthened its anti-discrimination unit), to actively explore ways of combating anti-Semitism more effectively in the future. All parts of the Secretariat should be vigilant. And of course — as always — we look to our friends in civil society to keep us up to the mark.

Sixty years since the first of the death camps were liberated by advancing Soviet forces, there could be no more fitting time for member states to take action on the necessity of combating anti-Semitism in all its forms — action comparable, perhaps, to the resolutions they adopted on apartheid in the past, or the admirable recent resolution of the Commission on Human Rights, which asked the Special Rapporteur on contemporary forms of racism to examine the situation of Muslim and Arab peoples in various parts of the world, with special reference to physical assaults and attacks against their places of worship, cultural centers, businesses and properties. Are not Jews entitled to the same degree of concern and protection?

Member states could follow the excellent lead of the Berlin Declaration, recently issued by the Chairman of the Organization for Security and Cooperation in Europe.

Let me remind you that the Declaration condemned without reserve all manifestations of anti-Semitism, and all other acts of intolerance, incitement, harassment, or violence against persons or communities based on ethnic origin or religious belief, wherever they occur.

The Declaration also condemned all attacks motivated by anti-Semitism or by any other forms of religious or racial hatred or intolerance, including attacks against synagogues and other religious places, sites and shrines.

And it declared unambiguously that international developments or political issues, including those in Israel or elsewhere in the Middle East, never justify anti-Semitism.

The Berlin Declaration proclaimed those principles, which I hope the broader membership of the United Nations will adopt. Even more important, it must make sure these principles are put into practice, and carefully monitor its own progress in doing so. The fight against anti-Semitism must be our fight. And Jews everywhere must feel that the United Nations is their home too.

We must make this vision a reality while we still have survivors of the Holocaust amongst us — like my dear friend Elie Wiesel. We owe them no less.

Let me conclude by quoting something Elie wrote:

"There is divine beauty in learning, just as there is human beauty in tolerance. To learn means to accept the postulate that life did not begin at my birth. Others have been here before me, and I walk in their footsteps. The books I have read were composed by generations of fathers and sons, mothers and daughters, teachers and disciples. I am the sum total of their experiences, their quests. And so are you."

An enormous Hitler support rally from Leni Riefenstahl's film,
"Triumph des Willens" ("Triumph of the Will")
1934

Eastern European children imprisoned behind barbed wire,
Auschwitz concentration camp
July 1944

Starved Jewish boys, Auschwitz-Birkenau
concentration camp
1944

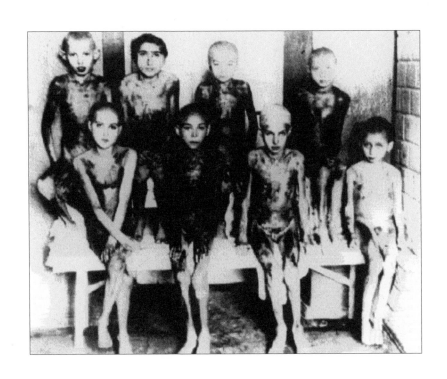

Poster from rally, New York City
April 2002

Cover of booklet distributed throughout the United
States by white supremist group, World Church of
the Creator (WCOTC)
March 2002

Poster charging that Jews control the U.S. government
and media, from a rally in Washington D.C.
April 2002

American Ku Klux Klan supporters

Four tattooed skinheads giving the "Heil Hitler" salute, their faces contorted into grimaces and hate

Flyer handed to UN delegates attending a conference in
South Africa by anti-Semitic NGO, Durban, South Africa
September 2001

What If I had Won?

the good things	the bad things
THERE WOULD BE **NO** ISRAEL AND **NO** PALESTINIAN'S BLOOD SHED	I WOULD'NT HAVE ALLOWED THE MAKING OF THE NEW BEETLE
THE REST IS YOUR GUESS	**THE REST IS YOUR GUESS**

Article from *Australian Jewish News*
March 1996

Swastikas on Melbourne homes

Margaret Safran

TWO properties in the Melbourne suburb of South Caulfield were daubed with swastikas and anti-Jewish graffiti last weekend.

The daubings occurred late Friday night or early Saturday morning.

Both properties were up for auction over the weekend and one had to be repainted before going to sale.

Real estate agent Lloyd Davis discovered the black paint daubings on Saturday morning when he went to put up an "auction today" flag at one of the properties. He was able to remove the daubed signs before the auction and contacted John Leske whose company, Leske, Cohen and Sandor, was auctioning another property on Sunday.

The building and auction signs at the latter property were extensively covered with swastikas and the statements "Jews get out" and "Jews go home" painted in large letters.

"I'm very angry about it. What worries me is that it can happen again," Mr Leske said.

Both Mr Leske and Mr Davis, who has worked as a real estate agent in Caulfield for 45 years, said it was their first personal experience of antisemitic daubings. They said they did not believe it had anything to do with an article on real estate on that street which appeared in the Australian Jewish News property section last week and which had referred to the two properties.

But newly appointed execu-

One of the houses in South Caulfield, Melbourne, which was daubed with antisemitic graffiti last weekend.

tive director of the B'nai B'rith Anti-Defamation Commission Danny Ben-Moshe believes the attack was probably prompted by the AJN story.

"There were a number of auction boards in the area, but only the two mentioned in the AJN were daubed," he said. "The wording of the daubing indicates an orchestrated response to the Jewish News article. Jews did not live in either home and there were no mezuzot on the doorposts. This helps explain why the graffiti is unlike other more random daubings which tend to employ Holocaust-relat-

ed statements and remarks such as 'Kill the Jews'."

The attacks were reported to Caulfield Police Station. Senior Sargent Neil Mathieson said they were "obviously by the same offender" as the paint, handwriting and phrases used were identical.

"Unfortunately, there is not a lot you can do in situations like this unless someone knows who the offender is," he said. "Antisemitic daubings are pretty unusual and don't happen very often. You only get two or three cases in a 12-month period."

Sergeant Mathieson said he

believed the offenders were probably "a couple of yahoos coming home drunk" who decided to use antisemitic graffiti. "Pro-Nazi types would have picked their target better (the owner of the second house is not Jewish) and probably gone for North Caulfield, where in some streets virtually every house is Jewish, rather than South Caulfield, where only about half the houses are Jewish."

Other local real estate agents agreed that antisemitic daubings were a rare occurrence.

Australia
June 2003

Pig with Kosher Stamp posted on WPWW "White Pride
Women" website with associated internet links
January 2001

It's not fit for a pig,
but it's fit for a Jew.

**Boycott all products that have a
secret Kosher Tax Stamp:**

Ⓚ Ⓤ PV

Pay no taxes to the Jews !

»National Symbols
» Regional Symbols
»Canadian Symbols
» Correspondence to manufacturers
» Correspondence with the USDA
»The Great Kosher Rip Off

Blood on prayer shawl, Istanbul, Turkey
November 2003

We Plead on Behalf of an Ancient People

ELIE WIESEL

AT THE END of his magnificent and disturbing novel called *The Plague,* Albert Camus issues a warning. His hero, the famous humanist, Dr. Rieux, who survived the death of many of his friends and adversaries, is now at the very end of the story, alone, walking in the city, remembering and listening to the cries of joy rising from the town.

And all of a sudden, says Camus, Rieux,
his hero, remembered:

"That such joy is always imperiled. He
knew what those jubilant crowds did not
know, but could have learned from books, that
the plague bacillus never dies or disappears for
good. That it can lie dormant for years and
years in furniture and linen chests, that it
bides its time in bedrooms, cellars, trunks and
bookshelves and that perhaps the day would
come when for the bane and the enlightening
of man it would rouse up its rats again and
send them forth to die in a happy city." And
that is also anti-Semitism.

We plead on behalf of an ancient PEOPLE
who, in some quarters, continues to be vilified,
threatened, offended and physically marked
for humiliation. Call it anti-Semitism or

Jew-hatred, it is the oldest collective bigotry in recorded history. In fact, one may say that of all the group-hatreds in antiquity, anti-Semitism alone survived antiquity. It is no longer political, social or religious: it is existential. Anti-Semitism is *sui generis.*

Other people, other traditions, other religious communities and cultures have been persecuted for a variety of reasons; anti-Semitism combines them all. The anti-Semite doesn't know me — but he hates me. Actually, he hated me even before I was born. He even hates the dead — otherwise why such sacrilege in so many profaned cemeteries?

A young Israeli visiting Berlin was assaulted in the street in broad daylight yesterday. Last week a young Jewish student was stabbed in Paris. A number of European

Jews told me that they live in fear. Incitement to hate and violence continues to fill the pages and the TV screens in many, too many, Muslim countries.

Under the pretext of blaming Israel's policies, which they outrageously exaggerate and demonize, their western allies and supporters encourage hatred towards the entire Jewish people. This is the first time in history that the United Nations has decided to explore the roots and consequences of a plague that has brought agony and distress to my people and shame to civilization itself.

Anti-Semitism used to be culturally fashionable and even socially permissible. Goethe detests the Bible, which he called a pugwash of Egypto-Babylonian sodomy. Augustine declared that Jews were still around so that Christians could see in them descendants of Cain and their sins.

Hegel said: "the Jewish people are servile, incapable of liberty; they cannot escape slavery except by enslaving others." On different levels, famous artists, renowned writers, would not hesitate to utter anti-Semitic remarks at cocktails or concerts. The kindest among them thought: just words, words; it doesn't mean anything.

Both amazing and intellectually disturbing is the realization that even renowned writers, thinkers and artists were infected by the anti-Jewish virus.

Richard Wagner and Louis-Ferdinand Céline remain inexplicable examples: how could artistic greatness co-exist with stupid and ferocious racist hatred? And

Hegel? Why did he state that: "The great tragedy of the Jewish people cannot but arouse disgust"?

Ezra Pound and Renoir, Kant and Dostoyevsky all had something unpleasant, something ugly, to say about Jews. And Schopenhauer, who violently denounced what he called "Jewish stink" everywhere they are? Why did he accuse the Jews of seeing their homeland only in other Jews? Why did Luther, who demonstrated extraordinary courage in defying Rome, produce such anti-Jewish diatribes and curses when he grew old?

Listen to Voltaire: "We find in the Jews an ignorant and barbarous people who have long united the most avarice with the most detestable superstition and the most invincible hatred for every people by whom they are tolerated and enriched…" Still, he added with magnanimity, "We ought not to burn them."

But now we know the consequences. We know that words can kill, just as they can heal. Anti-Semitism has even managed to penetrate the United Nations community. Had it not been for the courageous stance of moral leaders inside the United Nations organization, the infamous resolution comparing Zionism to racism would still be in effect. As for Durban, there efforts were less successful: instead of being a conference against hatred it became a conference of hatred.

The United Nations was created not only to put an end to aggression and war but also to protect innocent victims of fascism and Nazism — and I belong to a people that has been its principal target. Hence we turn to the United Nations and ask its leadership to fulfill its mission and use its political and moral authority to outlaw the plague that anti-Semitism is.

I have devoted most of my adult life to combating many evils of society: intolerance, bigotry, racism, fanaticism and indifference to other people's suffering and fears. But I never thought I would have to fight anti-Semitism. Naively I was convinced that it died in Auschwitz. Now I realize my mistake; it didn't. Only the Jews perished there. Anti-Semitism is alive and well in too many lands. Doesn't the organized world and its moral and intellectual leadership remember the consequences of anti-Semitism? Some of us endured them. We were there — we saw our parents and friends die — because of anti-Semitism.

Thus my plea to the Secretary-General. Help us fight it, help us disarm it. To do so would be in the interest of the United Nations for it would serve the cause of humanity at large. Hatred is contagious. It is a cancer. Who hates Jews, hates all minorities, all those who are different. Who hates Jews will end up hating everybody — and then himself.

In conclusion, I quote from the last page from a recent novel called *The Oath*. It is about a seventeenth century pogrom in an Eastern European shtetl. Hooligans set the Jewish quarter afire. Jewish homes were burning. But soon the flames invaded the Christian quarter as well. They were out to destroy Jews and ended up destroying themselves too.

"I was stepping back and back, but the distance remained unchanged. The prey of death, the price of life: Kolvillag was burning and I watched it burn. The House of Study, the trees and the walls — whipped by fire and wind. The cobblestones — shattered.

The Jewish quarter, the churches and the schools, the store and the warehouses: yellow and red, orange and purple flames escaped from them, only to return at once. The shelter and the orphanage, the tavern and the synagogue joined by a bridge of fire. The cemetery was burning, the police station was burning, the cribs were burning, the library was burning. On that night man's work yielded to the power and judgment of the fire. And suddenly I understood with every fiber of my being why I was shuddering at this vision of horror: I had just glimpsed the future.

"The Rebbe and his murderers, the sanctuary and its desecrators, the beggars and their stories, I trembled as I left them — left them, backing away. I saw them from afar, then I saw them no more. Only the fire still lived in what was once a town, mine. Charred dwellings. Charred corpses. Charred dreams and prayers and songs. Every story has an end, just as every end has a story. And yet, and yet. In the case of this city reduced to ashes, the two stories merge into one and remain a secret — such had been the will of my mad friend named Moshe, last prophet and teacher of a mankind that is no more."

In this 15th century woodcut, Jews are depicted murdering the child Simon of Trent. This "murder" is one of the sources of the medieval blood libel: the allegation that Jews used Christian children's blood to make matzoh (unleavened bread) during Passover. The Jews can be recognized by the circular patches sewn on their clothing and by the money bags they carry.

61

Cartoon depicting Jews from *Der Stürmer*, issue #37.
Original Title: Legion of Shame. Original Caption:
Ignorant, lured by gold—They stand disgraced in
Judah's fold. Souls poisoned, blood infected—Disaster
broods in their wombs, Germany
August 1935

Legion der Schande

Unaufgeklärt, verlockt vom Gold – Stehn sie, geschändet, in Judassold
Die Seelen vergiftet, verseucht das Blut – In ihrem Schoße das Unheil ruht

Cover of *Der Stürmer*, issue #9. Original Title:
The Mobilization of the People. The cartoon shows a
photograph of a Jew captioned "Satan." *Der Stürmer*
regularly used the old religious argument that the Jews
were in league with the Devil, Germany
February 1943

Desecration of synagogue, South Tottenham,
Great Britain
June 2004

Flyer from anti-Israel hate-fest at Rutgers University,
New Jersey
October 2003

Desecration of Jewish cemetery, south of France
November 2003

The cartoon's headline: The Feast of Immolation. On
the right, in Arabic: "The Islamic world's attitude?"

(Eid al-Adha, The Feast of Immolation, also called The
Festival of Sacrifice, is a 3-day festival commemorating
the Prophet Abraham's willingness to sacrifice his son,
Ishmael, in obedience to God. After a morning of communal
prayer, Muslims slaughter an animal to signify the angel
Gabriel's substitution of a lamb to fulfill Abraham's
sacrificial obligation.)
Al-Watan newspaper, Oman
February 3, 2004

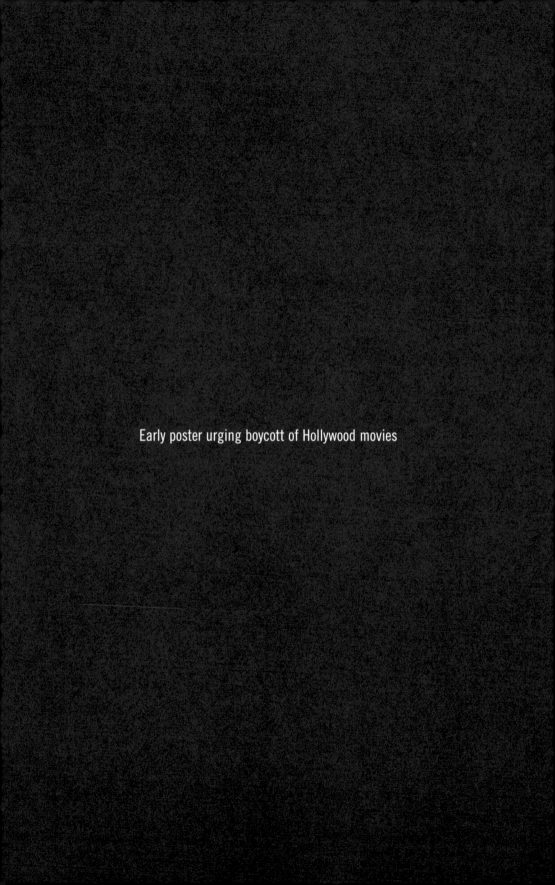
Early poster urging boycott of Hollywood movies

Vandalized memorial to Jewish soldiers who died in the
Battle of Verdun, France
May 2004

Church sign using a biblical citation to blame Jews for the death of Jesus, Denver, Colorado

Bag of explosives, Great Britain
October 2003

Contemporary Italian wine bottles with images of
Hitler and Mussolini, Italy
May 2003

Wolf with *Magen David* on the way to kill sheep,
Al-Riyadh newspaper, Saudi Arabia
September 2001

Covers from various editions of
"Protocols of the Elders of Zion" a fraudulent
document widely used as a rationale for
anti-Semitism.
(Clockwise from top left)
Spain, 1930
France, 1934
Poland, 1943
Egypt, 1972
United Kingdom, 1978
Russia, 1992